THE NO NONSENSE LIBRARY

NO NONSENSE CAREER GUIDES:

How to Choose a Career
How to Re-Enter the Workforce
How to Use Your Time Wisely
How to Write a Resume
Managing People At Work/At Home
No Nonsense Interviewing

OTHER NO NONSENSE GUIDES:

Car Guides
Cooking Guides
Financial Guides
Health Guides
Legal Guides
Parenting Guides
Photography Guides
Real Estate Guides
Study Guides
Success Guides
Wine Guides

NO NONSENSE CAREER GUIDE®

HOW TO CHOOSE A CAREER

Beatryce Nivens

Longmeadow Press

To my mother, Surluta Nivens,
who helped enormously with
the writing of this book.

This publication is designed to provide accurate and
authoritative information with regard to the subject matter
covered. It is sold with the understanding that neither the
publisher nor the authors are engaged in rendering legal,
accounting, or other professional service regarding the subject
matter covered. If legal advice or other expert assistance is
desired, the services of a competent professional should be
sought.

TABLE OF CONTENTS

TABLES LIST

ACKNOWLEDGMENTS

Writing a book is never easy. I would like to thank the following people for their assistance in making this an easier task:

Marie Brown, who encouraged me to write this book, and gave invaluable assistance in developing it.

Elza Dinwiddie Boyd, my colleague, who supported the idea that I should write this book.

Tracy A. Sherrod, who was a researcher.

The Department of Labor, Bureau of Labor Statistics that has published two very fine books which were resources for this book: *The Occupational Outlook Handbook* and *The Dictionary of Occupational Titles*.

INTRODUCTION

Have you longed for career happiness? Have you decided that life is short and you want to make the most of your work life? Or does your career "bio" read: "unhappy with life, my company, and co-workers. Can hardly drag out of bed to go to work. Complain bitterly about everything and everyone at work. Wish I could leave, but it's the security." Perhaps it reads: "I've been out of the job market for several years and have no skills or work achievements. Guess no one would want *me*!" Or does it say: "I'm just a college student. Everyone knows you have to wait until you get in the 'real world' to get skills or valid work experience."

Everyone has been a little unhappy with his or her career choice. However, it takes a determined person to do something about it. Or are you one of the unbelievers who thinks working is a life sentence with no privileges. Do you really feel you can move into the perfect career? Or are you complacent about achieving career happiness?

If you've decided you can change your life and find career happiness, you will greatly benefit from the *How To Choose a Career*. In this book, you will explore up-to-the minute career planning/job search techniques: goal setting, analyzing your skills and work achievements; organizing your career research; mapping your own job search campaign; writing a marketable resume and cover letter. You will get a great deal of the needed information to successfully propel yourself into a new career.

However, you must be willing to work hard to achieve your dreams. After all, there is nothing easy in life. So, get ready, set, and start moving toward your career happiness.

RECLAIMING YOUR CAREER DREAMS

Reclaim your career happiness by looking at how you landed in your present career. If you are presently in the job market, some of you needed fast money to pay your bills, and haphazardly chose a job. If you are a college student, perhaps your security-oriented parents insisted that you pursue a certain career path. If you are a career changer, you have undoubtedly found it impossible to happily settle into your career, but don't know where to go.

Today, most people suffer from various forms of career unhappiness. Some suffer silently; others constantly bicker and complain about their jobs; still others develop work-related stress and health disorders from unhappy work situations. And all of this career unhappiness stems from the failure of people to choose the right careers.

But how do you get on the right career path? There are basically three ways to uncover it: 1. assessing your childhood dreams; 2. analyzing your school likes and peeves; 3. going for career counseling and testing.

By assessing your childhood career dreams, you can learn a great deal about your future career happiness.

Once, a long time ago, your career dreams indicated what type of work person you hoped to become: a helper of others; money-maker, mega-business mover and shaker; benefactor to your community and its residents; artistic genius.

Although many people deny that they had any childhood career dreams, we all did. However, in many cases, these dreams were discouraged by well-meaning parents, teachers, counselors, relatives, employers, and others. For some of you, these discouraging words were devastating and permanently disconnected you from your true career selves.

Most of us have experienced these words of career discouragment: "girls can't be engineers;" "musicians don't make enough money;" "get a secure government job;" "you're not smart enought to be a doctor;" "your future career doesn't pay enough money;" "you're too old." Does any of this sound familiar? Have these negative thoughts conditioned and discouraged you? Perhaps you can't even remember what you originally wanted to do.

But how can you reclaim your childhood career dreams? Start by remembering what you wanted to become as an adult. Did you want to be a nurse, doctor, lawyer, librarian, dancer, accountant, astronaut, scientist, or other professional? Be honest! Although this may seem like a very simple exercise, career counselors have used this technique to help unearth a person's original career desires, and set them on a path to true career happiness. After all, your childhood career goals came from the heart, were honest and untarnished by other people's opinions. So, again, what was your original career dream?

If you have been honest, you can now assess what your childhood dreams said about your career hopes and aspirations. If you wanted to become a doctor or teacher or other helping professional, you had a strong desire to assist others. If being an astronaut stimulated you, you have an adventurous spirit and perhaps shouldn't be confined to a nine to five job. If you set your eyes on a scientific career, you are probably research oriented and needed to work in an environment that nourishes this need. If Hollywood beckoned you, you are creative and need a work environment where you can be imaginative. If you were a childhood artist, you don't need a career that stifles your creative genius or one that is repetitive and boring.

Another way to determine your best career choice is to look at your joys and peeves in school. If you didn't like or can't do well in math as a student, you probably won't like a career in engineering or computer science or actuarial science. If you couldn't pass Speech 101, you are probably petrified of speaking in front of groups and won't enjoy a career as a trainer, lecturer or teacher. If Psychology 100 bored you, you won't have enough enthusiasm to struggle through graduate psychology studies. If English composition stumped you, you shouldn't be attracted to a career that demands a great deal of writing, such as law.

Although you can overcome your difficulties in a subject area or major, it is important to determine which were your problem areas. For example, a person who can't stomach cutting a frog in Biology 101, will probably have difficulties as a surgeon, but may excel in another career. Listen to your inner feelings in regards to your likes and pet peeves for school subjects. They may save you many years of working in a career that doesn't suit you.

If you are still having trouble determining what career will make you happy, it may be time to get professional help from a private career counselor. A career counselor can help you discover some of yor career interests by giving you one or more career interest inventory tests like the Strong-Campbell or the self scoring Self-Directed Search, but ask about the benefits of each test. You may also want your counselor to help you use Discover, a computer program that assists you in researching various careers and job search information.

If you can't find or afford a private career counselor,

you can get testing and career counseling from your high school guidance counselor, college or university career planning/placement counselors, staffers at community or private agencies. Or you may get help at one of the 2,000 state employment service offices (Job Service) which work in conjunction with the Labor Department's US Employment Service. To find an office nearest you, look in your telephone book under "Job Service" or "Employment." For a listing of accredited counseling services in your area, get the International Association for Counseling Services' (IACS) *Directory of Counseling Services*. IACS' address is 5999 Stevenson Avenue, Alexandria, Virginia 22304.

The following organizations can also provide career information and make referrals for specific groups:

1. For the Handicapped:

President's Committee on Employment
  of the Handicapped
1111 20th Street, N.W., Room 636
Washington, D.C. 20036

2. For the Blind:

Call the Job Opportunities for the Blind
  Program (National Federation for the
Blind)
1-800-638-7518

3. For Minorities:

a. League of United Latin American Citizens
   (LULAC)
National Education Service Centers
400 First Street, N.W., Suite 716
Washington, D.C. 20001

b. National Urban League
Employment Department
500 E. 62nd Street
New York, New York 10021

4. Older Workers:

National Association of Older Workers
   Employment Services
c/o National Council on Aging
600 Maryland Avenue, S.W.
Washington, D.C. 20024

2

DECLARING YOUR GOALS

Your ultimate or major career goal is your future position, and mini-goals will help keep you on track to accomplishing this ultimate career dream. Most achievers set goals and inch towards them in a methodical way.

What are your goals? What is your future or ultimate career goal? Do you want to be an accountant, bank officer, buyer, city manager, construction worker, health services administrator, personnel manager, purchasing agent, architect, teacher, engineer, social worker, psychologist, scientist, economist, or other worker? How will you accomplish this dream?

Sometimes major career goals can be overwhelming. When they are, it is best to make mini-goals. Let's say that you are a male or female high school graduate in your late twenties and want to become a physician. This big dream can take as long as fifteen years to achieve. To keep from being overwhelmed by this dream, you should break your goals into mini-goals. For example, your first goal might be to complete an associate's degree program in biology at your local community or junior college. A second one would be to transfer to a four-year college or university to complete your pre-med studies. Your third goal would be to get accepted to and attend medical school. Your ultimate goal would be to finish medical school and complete post-medical school studies.

These mini-goals can be broken into three areas: short-term, median and long-term. Short-term goals are from right now until a year from now; median ones are from one year to five years; long-term goals can take from five years until the end of your work life.

In the case of the man or woman who wants to become a physician, short-term goals might be to get academic and financial aid information from a local community or junior college, then apply and get accepted to the school, and begin his or her studies. His or her median goals could include getting an associate's degree; transferring to a four-year college or university, and completing his or her pre-med studies. If he or she stays on target, he or she can get a bachelor's degree in five years or less.

In the next four years, he or she should be able to complete four years of medical school. In another one or two years, he or she can take a supervised practice in an accredited graduate medical education program (residency) and become eligible for licensing as a full-fledged physician.

In **Table 1** make a list of your goals or plans. Remember, as you go along in life, these goals can be changed.

TABLE 1

GOAL SETTING MAP

MY ULTIMATE CAREER GOAL IS _____

I WILL ACCOMPLISH THIS BY _____

1. *My short-term or present goals:* _____

_____

_____

_____

_____

2. *What can I do right now to help me accomplish these goals?* _____

_____

_____

_____

_____

3. *My median goals:* _____

_____

_____

_____

_____

_____

4. *What can I do right now or in the future to accomplish these goals?* _____

_____

_____

_____

_____

_____

5. *My long-term or ultimate goal:* _____

_____

_____

_____

_____

6. *What can I do now or in the near or distant future to help me accomplish this?* _____

_____

_____

_____

_____

_____

3

WHAT'S IN YOUR SKILLS BANK?

What are skills? Skills are things that you do well in paid and non-paid work, internships, parenting, life, etc. Some skills are learned. Others are talents like singing, playing an instrument, creative writing, etc.

Knowing your skills can open new career possibilities. However, most people aren't aware of their many skills. In this chapter, you will learn how to determine your skills by looking at general skills that you have learned through work and life experiences.

Because most people are not in touch with their skills, they undersell themselves in the workplace. Many people look at their job titles and feel these designations say what they do for a living. However, career counselors have found that many people have acquired skills far beyond the descriptions of their job titles. For example, a secretary may actually be a human resources manager. Or a counselor may be an administrator. Or an editorial assistant may be a writer. Or an office manager may actually be running a company.

Skills awareness will help you feel good about yourself

and see new career possibilities. And if you know your skills, you can create a marketable resume that will help open career doors.

Whether you are in high school, college, or in the process of changing careers, you have skills that will make you a valuable employee. Let's begin by looking at **Table 2** and taking inventory of your general skills. After completing this exercise, do you now have some idea of the many things that you can do? In the next three chapters, you will discover your hidden and transferable skills.

TABLE 2

GENERAL SKILLS
(Check The Skills That You Have)

I CAN

- ☐ Accomplish and finish projects
- ☐ Adapt to new situations
- ☐ Address envelopes
- ☐ Administer programs, projects, etc.
- ☐ Advise others
- ☐ Advocate for others
- ☐ Analyze problems
- ☐ Appraise situations
- ☐ Make approvals for ideas or projects
- ☐ Arrange merchandise and products
- ☐ Assemble things
- ☐ Assign tasks to others
- ☐ Audit individuals, departments, companies or organizations
- ☐ Perform bookkeeping tasks
- ☐ Prepare budgets for my company
- ☐ Build things
- ☐ Brainstorm with others
- ☐ Calculate numbers using a calculator
- ☐ Care for others
- ☐ Cater for parties or other events
- ☐ Classify information
- ☐ Coach others to be successful
- ☐ Collect money or information from others
- ☐ Communicate well orally or in writing
- ☐ Compile information
- ☐ Compose music

- ☐ Use a computer
- ☐ Conceive of ideas and projects
- ☐ Conduct business in a professional manner
- ☐ Do consulting work in my field
- ☐ Contribute ideas, manpower, etc. to my organization
- ☐ Cook
- ☐ Cooperate with others to get the job done
- ☐ Counsel others
- ☐ Create things
- ☐ Criticize others in a constructive way
- ☐ Dance
- ☐ Debate others
- ☐ Make decisions in a timely way
- ☐ Deliver work on time
- ☐ Demonstrate products or things to prospective customers
- ☐ Design
- ☐ Diagnose illness or other problems
- ☐ Discuss things with others
- ☐ Discipline self to get the job done
- ☐ Display products
- ☐ Distribute material or products to others
- ☐ Do detail work
- ☐ Develop ideas, projects, etc.
- ☐ Direct others
- ☐ Draft
- ☐ Draw

- ☐ Edit books, articles, and other communication materials
- ☐ Educate others
- ☐ Enforce rules or regulations
- ☐ Enlist others to perform tasks
- ☐ Evaluate
- ☐ Examine documents and other materials
- ☐ Facilitate groups
- ☐ File
- ☐ Fund raise
- ☐ Handle complaints
- ☐ Identify problems
- ☐ Index information
- ☐ Inspect things like facilities or instruments
- ☐ Interview individuals or groups
- ☐ Invent products
- ☐ Keep records
- ☐ Lead others
- ☐ Learn quickly
- ☐ Listen well
- ☐ Make layouts
- ☐ Measure things
- ☐ Mechanically reason
- ☐ Memorize numbers, information, etc.
- ☐ Motivate others
- ☐ Negotiate with others
- ☐ Utilize nursing skills
- ☐ Observe places, people, and things
- ☐ Obtain information
- ☐ Order merchandise
- ☐ Organize my work
- ☐ Paint

- ☐ Perservere
- ☐ Persuade others to act
- ☐ Plan
- ☐ Prioritize
- ☐ Process information quickly
- ☐ Promote events
- ☐ Proofread
- ☐ Purchase products, materials, etc.
- ☐ Write poems
- ☐ Record information
- ☐ Recruit people
- ☐ Research
- ☐ Rewrite reports
- ☐ Schedule appointments
- ☐ Take risks
- ☐ Take shorthand
- ☐ Simplify things
- ☐ Sing
- ☐ Solve problems
- ☐ Stimulate others
- ☐ Summarize materials
- ☐ Supervise others
- ☐ Be a team player
- ☐ Train others
- ☐ Type
- ☐ Update reports
- ☐ Use instruments
- ☐ Work with others
- ☐ Write grants
- ☐ Write magazine or newspaper articles
- ☐ Write technical materials
- ☐ Write screenplays
- ☐ Write poems

4

LOCATING YOUR HIDDEN SKILLS

Many of you have hidden skills. As a result of working beyond your job title, you have acquired a wide variety of "hidden" skills in the process. One way to uncover these skills is to closely look at what you do at your job.

Let's use the example of the secretary to see how to uncover your hidden skills. By looking at one of the secretary's job duties in **Table 3**, you can see the number of skills used to perform that one duty. If this secretary expands his or her list to include ten or eleven job duties, she or he may uncover one hundred or more skills.

Let's uncover your hidden skills. Make a list of job duties that you perform at your present job. If you are unsure, make a daily log of all your duties for a week by jotting down what you do from nine to five. Once you know the duties, think about what skills you use to perform each duty. Use **Table 3** as a guide.

After you finish, do the same for every job that you have held. If you feel ambitious, do the same for volunteer work or internships. It is very important to complete this

14

exercise because you will need this information to properly write your resume.

Look at the results of your skills exercise and pat yourself on the back. "Don't you have more skills than you originally thought?"

TABLE 3

HOW TO UNCOVER YOUR HIDDEN SKILLS

JOB TITLE: Secretary

One Job Duty: Answering the telephone for ABC Company (When I carefully look at my first job duty, I am using the following skills to perform that duty):

By answering the telephone, I
__ Have good public relations skills
__ Am enthusiastic about the day and project that happiness to customers
__ Am a resource person who knows where everyone in the company is located, their telephone extensions and room numbers
__ Am able to communicate well orally
__ Am able to take messages correctly
__ Can take messages in shorthand and rewrite them for the people who will receive them
__ Am able to give messages to people in a prompt and timely manner
__ Can summarize messages, but get information correctly
__ Am able to do light typing and filing when needed
__ Have good listening skills
__ Can route information in a timely manner

__ Am able to greet guests on the telephone in a cheerful manner and make them feel comfortable

__ Am well organized

__ Can make decisions regarding telephone calls

__ Can perform more than one task at a time *i.e.* answer telephone, put someone on hold, take a message, type a note, etc.

__ Am a problem solver when things go wrong at the front desk

__ Am a good team player because my position demands it

__ Can listen to customer complaints and refer them to the correct person to handle them

__ Am a keen observer of people, things, and places

__ Am good at obtaining information

__ Can follow through and get the job done

__ Can prioritize tasks

__ Am good at recognizing problems and trying to resolve them

__ Can make appointments with regard to others' schedules, priorities, and demands

__ Can interview people as to what they want and who they should ultimately see or talk with

__ **TOTAL NUMBER OF SKILLS FOR DUTY OF ANSWERING THE TELEPHONE**

5

UNEARTHING YOUR TRANSFERABLE SKILLS

What are transferable skills? They are your skills that can be transferred to another career. Many of you have a great many transferable skills, but may not know what they are or their transferability to another career area.

To begin to know your transferable skills, you must first identify what skills are needed for your new career. To help, use the *Dictionary of Occupational Titles* (US Department of Labor, Employment and Training Administration) which should be available in your local library. Look up your job title and determine the skills needed to perform the work. For example, let's say that you plan to become an *employment interviewer* for a human resources department of an organization. The D.O.T. lists the following skills for this position:

- Interviews job applicant to select persons meeting employer's qualifications;

- Reviews completed applications and evaluates applicant's work history, education and training, job skills,

salary desired, and physical and personal qualifications;

- Records additional skills, knowledge, abilities, interests, test results, and other data pertinent to classifi-
cation, selection, and referral;

- Searches files of job orders from employers and
matches applicant's qualifications with job requirements and employer specifications, utilizing manual
file search, computer matching services or employment service facilities;

- Informs applicant about job duties and responsibilities, pay and benefits, hours and working conditions,
company and union policies, promotional opportunities, and other related information;

- Refers selected applicants to interview with person
placing job order according to policy of school, agency
or company;

- Keeps for future reference records of applicants not
immediatley selected or hired;

- Performs reference or background checks;

- May test or arrange for skills, intelligence or psychological testing of applicant;

- May engage in research or follow-up activities to
evaluate selection and placement techniques by con-
ferring with management and supervisory personnel;

- May specialize in interviewing and referring certain
types of personnel such as professional, technical,

managerial, clerical and other types of skilled or unskilled workers.

Once you have looked in the *Dictionary of Occupational Titles* and determined the skills used in your future career, write them on a piece of paper and check off which skills you have. Keep this for later use in developing your resume.

In this and the previous chapters, you have learned your general, hidden, and transferable skills. In future chapters, you will learn how to use these skills to write a marketable resume. But first, let's discover your work achievements.

6

FINDING YOUR WORK ACHIEVEMENTS

Whether you've worked full-time or part-time, in paid or non-paid (volunteer or civic) work or internships, you have work achievements. Most of you may be saying: "I didn't achieve anything at any of my jobs." However, after closely inspecting your experiences, you will learn to discover your achievements.

What are work achievements? They are things that you have done to increase profits or efficiency, or benefit your company or organization. One work achievement for someone in a paid position may be that he or she wrote a training manual to help teachers work with handicapped children. As a result, these children increased their reading or math scores by 50%. Another achievement could be the development of a log to chronicle incoming and outgoing mail. This resulted in helping your company keep track of mail which increased bill collections by 35%.

As a volunteer fund raiser, you may have raised $125,000 for your organization by designing attractive fliers and brochures and motivating other volunteers to sell chance books, etc. Or, as a student intern for an insurance company, you created a filing system that helped claims agents more efficiently process claims.

On the left, in **Table 4**, write down your job or position titles (paid and non-paid positions). In column two, write down your major job duties, and in the next column, your work achievements. For future use, you should also determine what prompted you to make these achievements. For example, if one of your achievements is that you designed a filing system, why did you do this? Did it take your co-workers too long to locate documents? Did you want to increase your department's efficiency?

TABLE 4

WORK ACHIEVEMENTS		
Jobs or positions: (Paid, Non-paid, etc.)	*My Job Duties*	*My Work Achievements*
1.		
2.		
3.		
4.		
5.		
6.		
7.		
8.		
9.		
10.		

7

ORGANIZING YOUR CAREER RESEARCH

By now, you have unearthed your career dreams, set goals, analyzed your skills, and determined your work achievements. It is now time to research your future career by contacting professional associations, reading career books, and talking to people in your future career area.

Professional Associations

Nearly every field has a professional association that fosters professional development for its members. However, many of these groups are interested in attracting newcomers to the field, and have developed free or low cost career information. Some of this information includes national salary surveys, descriptions of positions, skills needed for the field, training opportunities, scholarships, etc. This information can be invaluable in your job search.

If you want to network with people in, or learn more about your career, most professional associations have local chapters in a number of cities, and will allow non-members to attend meetings. These organizations also have national conventions or conferences. Again, you can learn about your future field and meet people who work in it. Another benefit of attending a professional association's convention is that employers often come there to recruit. Even if you don't get a job at the convention, you can make contacts for the future.

If you plan to get additional education in your future field, some professional associations offer scholarships. These financial bonanzas are usually not publicized and are only available by contacting the association. For example, the American Psychological Association offers minority fellowships for those who want to pursue graduate study in the field. To contact a professional association in your future field, ask your local librarian for *The Encyclopedia of Associations* (Gale Press).

Reading About Your Career

One of the best ways to learn about your career is to read career books and other materials. There is one book that is helpful in your career research: *The Occupational Outlook Handbook* which is published by the Department of Labor, Bureau of Labor Statistics, and is available at your local library or from the Superintendent of Documents, US Government Printing Office, Washington, D.C. 20402. This book gives information on 200 occupations: nature of the work; working conditions; employment; training, other qualifications and advancement; job outlook; earnings; related occupations; sources of additional information.

There are also many career books on the market which explore topics from launching a career, to the actual job search, to resume writing and interviewing techniques. For a partial list see *Appendix A.*

You may gain a great deal from reading career articles in magazines and newspapers. Magazines like *Working*

Woman, Working Mother, Black Enterprise, and others specialize in career information. Periodically, you can find career articles in some of the following publications: *Business Week, Forbes, Time, Newsweek, Venture Inc., Fortune,* etc. Don't forget to look at newspaper articles that may contain information about your future field. Ask for your librarian's help in locating both magazine and newspaper articles.

Most professional associations publish professional journals and trade magazines which are good sources of career information. Some of these journals and trade magazines include: *Data Communications, Advertising Age, Chronicle for Higher Education, Art Direction, ABA Banking Journal, Architectural Record, Chemical Weekly,* National Association of Female Executive's *Executive Woman.*

There are also industry newsletters which can provide valuable information about certain fields. Ask your librarian for the *Newsletter Directory* (Gale Research, Detroit, Michigan) and determine which is the best newsletter for you.

Talking To People In The Field

Do you know anyone or someone who knows someone in your future career? If so, either in person or by telephone, talk to this person about your selected field. These talks can be very revealing. For instance, one woman who wants to go into the social work field talked to several social workers. In these conversations, she found that social workers are faced with completing large amounts of paper work and have a great deal of on-the-job stress. As a result of these revelations, she has started to investigate other careers where she can also help people.

Talking to people in your field can reveal information that is not written in career books or magazine or newspaper articles. You can find out the daily ins and outs of a career, various career opportunities, salaries, the best companies to work for, etc.

After you have spoken to one person in your future career, ask for a referral to another person. Talk to as many people as possible to get a balanced view of the career. Although this may take a great deal of effort and time, you'll be surprised at what you'll learn.

8

FAST GROWING CAREERS THROUGH THE YEAR 2000

Since a vital part of career planning is surveying different options within each field, it is important for you to have information about your future career area. Below is career information on selected fields that the Department of Labor predicts has faster than average growth through the year 2000. For information on other career areas, refer to the *Occupational Outlook Handbook* (Department of Labor, Bureau of Labor Statistics).

1. COMPUTER PROGRAMMER

The technological revolution is exploding and computers are an integral part of this phenomenon. Contrary to what many people think, computers are machines, can't think, and must be told what to do. To do the desired work, they must be programmed by professionals known as computer programmers, who write programs, or logical step-by-step instructions, that tell the computer to perform certain duties. For example, a word processing program would allow a worker to perform typing duties such as creating a letter or document, making envelope labels, etc.

Computer programmers follow the instructions of systems analysts who are the computer department's liaisons, and have determined the needs of those requesting the programs or computer services.

They can work for government agencies, manufacturers, banks, colleges and universities, or insurance companies. Programmers can specialize in business applications for businesses or scientific applications for science oriented or engineering concerns. To do this job, you should be a logical thinker, be able to grasp abstract concepts, and have the ability to do technical analysis.

Education And Training

Computer programmers have various backgrounds. Some have college degrees from four-year colleges or universities; others have associate degrees from junior or community colleges; still others have been trained in vocational schools. However, since competition for these jobs is keen, employers are, increasingly, selecting college graduates to fill them.

If you are in college, course selection will depend upon which type of programming you want to do. For example, if you want to do business programming, your employer probably would like to see college courses in business and programming. On the other hand, a scientific or engineering programming job might require college majors in computer or information science, mathematics, engineering, or the physical sciences.

If you want to obtain some level of experiential and professional competence in the field, you can obtain the Certificate in Computer Programming (CCP) which is conferred by the Institute for Certification of Computer Professionals, and is awarded after you pass a core examination plus exams in two specialty areas.

Salaries

Recruiting Trends 1989-90 by L. Patrick Scheetz of Michigan State University reported that estimated starting salaries for June 1990 computer science graduates with bachelor's degrees was $27,707. The *Occupational Outlook Handbook* summarized that median earnings of full-time programmers were $30,600 a year in 1989.

For more information concerning certification of computer programmers, contact:
1. Institute for Certification of
   Computer Professionals
   2200 East Devon Avenue, Suite 268
   Des Plaines, Illinois 60018

2. COMPUTER SERVICE TECHNICIANS

Since computers play such a crucial role in today's society, their installation and maintenance is vital, and the workers who perform these duties—computer service technicians—are in demand. In fact, the Department of Labor ranks this career the fifth fastest growing occupation.

Computer service technicians keep computers and their peripheral equipment in tip-top working order. From desk-top computers to large systems, these service workers can travel from client to client to install, help maintain or do repairs on these machines. They can specialize in providing care for a certain type or brand of machine, or a particular type of repair.

These computer specialists must be savvy and have a good people skills; they can come in contact with different levels of company personnel, from the boss or top management person, to the secretary. In fact, they may be the only people who are in constant contact with a client, or who can tell the client of additional needed equipment. So, they often perform public relations and sales functions.

Education And Training

If you want to become a computer service technician, you should take a one- or two-year, post-high school training course in basic electronics, computer mainte- nance, or electrical engineering at a vocational school or community or junior college. However, some high school graduates are hired for these jobs. Once hired, you will probably have to take a six-month to two-year training program at work. Because the computer field and its equipment is constantly changing, you should take addi- tional continuing education courses in the field.

Salaries

According to the *Occupational Outlook Handbook*, the median yearly salaries for computer service technicians were approximately $26,700 in 1988.

For more information contact the human resources departments of computer manufacturers and computer maintenance firms.

3. PARALEGALS OR LEGAL ASSISTANTS

The Department of Labor ranks the paralegal field the number one fastest growing occupation through the year 2000. These professionals work under the supervision of lawyers and can perform research, do background and investigative work, prepare written reports, and give legal arguments, etc. A paralegal or legal assistant may help write documents like separation agreements, mortgages, or other contracts.

Employers of paralegals or legal assistants determine

the scope of their work. For example, one who works for a government agency has responsibilities according to the mission of the agency. If a paralegal or legal assistant works for a public defender or community law agency, and the law permits, he or she may represent clients at certain proceedings such as administrative social security disability hearings.

Some of these workers specialize in real estate, labor law, family law, litigation, estate planning, or corporate law. Most work for corporations, law firms, or government agencies.

Education And Training

Many paralegals or legal assistants have entered the field in various ways, including being trained by a supervising lawyer. However, many employers now expect that paralegals be formally trained in programs at colleges and universities, community and junior colleges, business schools, proprietary schools, legal assistant associations, etc. The American Bar Association has approved about **130** of the **600** nationwide paralegal training programs.

The admissions requirements to legal assistance programs vary. Some require college courses or a college degree; others will admit high school graduates or those with prior legal training. Completion of these programs vary anywhere from a few months to two or four years. Since competition is keen for legal assistant positions, you should best prepare yourself for the job market by enrolling in programs that will make you marketable.

There is also a certification processs for paralegals which is handled by the National Association of Legal Assistants and includes various educational and work experience requirements. To be eligible for the Certified Legal Assistant (CLA) credential, you must meet the established standards of the National Association of Legal Assistants, and pass a two-day examination that is given by the Certifying Board of Legal Assistants of the National Association of Legal Assistants.

Salaries

Earnings for paralegals vary depending upon training, work background, geographic location, and type of employer. A utilization and compensation survey by the National Association of Legal Assistants (*Occupational Outlook Handbook*) determined that average salaries for paralegals were $24,900 in 1988. Those workers with ten years of experience had average annual earnings of $28,500.

For more information contact:
1. National Association of Legal Assistants, Inc.
   1601 South Main Street, Suite 300
   Tulsa, Oklahoma 74119
2. National Federation of Paralegal Associations, Inc.
   104 Wilmot Road, Suite 201
   Deerfield, Illinois 60015-5195

For information regarding approved American Bar Association schools, contact:
3. Standing Committee on Legal Assistants
   American Bar Association
   750 North Lake Shore Drive
   Chicago, Illinois 60611

4. NURSES

There is a critical need for nurses that has created a demand for registered nurses (RN's), and the Department of Labor predicts excellent job prospects in the field. The greatest opportunities and salary incentives will be for nurse anesthetists.

Nurses work in hospitals, nursing homes, for private

clients, corporations, schools, unions, government agencies, in their own practices, as nurse practitioners, or for community health organizations. They can work full-time or part-time, or as per diem employees. They can also travel from hospital to hospital. They assist physicians in observing symptoms and reactions, preparing for examinations or operations, administering medicines, and helping patients in the recovery process by instructing them and/or their families on post-illness care procedures.

Education And Training

Nurses must be licensed to perform their duties. To become licensed, you must graduate from an approved nursing school and pass a national examination which is administered by each state.

Approved nursing programs are offered at junior or community colleges, hospitals, or colleges and universities. Depending on the program, it will take you from two to five years to complete. Obviously, the more formalized nursing education you have, the higher you will rise on the career ladder, and the more diversity you will have in practice specialties. However, you can take additional course work that will prepare you for higher level work. For example, if you complete an associate's degree in nursing at a junior or community college, you can transfer your credits to a college or university to earn a bachelor's degree. Because of the dynamic nature of the health and nursing field, it is also wise to consistently take continuing education courses to keep you abreast of these changes.

Salaries

The *Occupational Outlook Handbook* reported that, according to a University of Texas Medical Branch survey, starting salaries for staff hospital nurses averaged between $23,100 and $35,500 for nurse anesthetists. Experienced staff RN's averaged $32,100; head nurses made average salaries of $40,800; experienced nurse anesthetists averaged $52,700.

For more information, contact:

1. National League for Nursing
   Communications Department
   350 Hudson Street
   New York, New York 10014
2. American Nurses' Association
   2420 Pershing Road
   Kansas City, Missouri 64108
3. American Hospital Association

   Division of Nursing
   840 North Lake Shore Drive
   Chicago, Illinois 60611
4. American Health Care Association
   1201 L. Street, N.W.
   Washington, D.C. 20005
   (ask for a copy of *Health Careers in Long-Term Care*)

5. PHYSICAL THERAPISTS

If you have had a disabling injury or disease, you probably came in contact with a physical therapist who helped you get back on the road to recovery. These professionals, who work in the eighth-ranked fastest-growing occupation, help design and administer a treatment plan to relieve pain, restore functional mobility and prevent permanent disabilities for accident, stroke, sports injury, heart disease, arthritis, multiple sclerosis, amputation, nerve injury, or fracture victims. Through evaluation and testing, they are able to help patients regain muscle strength, mobility, and physical skills.

The field offers its workers opportunities to have their own practices, work for a group practice or consulting group. In fact, in 23 states, physical therapists can treat patients without physicians' referrals.

Education And Training

If you want to become a physical therapist, you must be licensed to perform your duties. To become licensed, you must have a degree or certificate from an accredited physical therapy program and pass a licensure examination. The educational path for physical therapists includes several options: graduation from a baccalaureate program in physical therapy, completion of a certificate program for those who already have a bachelor's degree in another field, or completion of a master's degree program in the field.

Salaries

According to the *Occupational Outlook Handbook* which quoted a national survey by the University of Texas' Medical Branch, starting salaries for entry-level, hospital-based physical therapy graduates averaged about $25,000 in 1989; those with experience averaged about $33,400.

For more information, contact:

1. American Physical Therapy Association
   1111 North Fairfax Street
   Alexandria, Virginia 22314

6. HOTEL MANAGERS, ASSISTANTS, AND OTHER WORKERS

The hotel industry is quickly becoming one of the fastest growing industries. As business travel increases and tourism grows, hotels are popping up across the country and in other parts of the world. As the population grows older and retires, these retirees often spend more leisure time traveling and staying at hotels, and this has contributed to the hotel industry's growth. Indications are that more and more Americans will cherish and spend more time in leisure pursuits which will also mean a healthy hotel industry. The Department of Labor, in fact, reports that employment prospects are expected to grow faster than average for hotel managers and assistants through the year 2000.

Education And Training

Many hotel managers and assistants have learned on the job and moved up the hotel hierarchy. However, many employers now prefer college or junior or community college graduates for these positions. To get a degree in hotel management, there are more than 150 colleges and universities that offer four-year degree or graduate programs in the field. Also, there are over 600 certificate programs offered by junior or community colleges, or technical schools. Some large hotel chains offer on-the-job management training programs.

Salaries

In an American Hotel and Motel Association survey that was quoted in the *Occupational Outlook Handbook*, reported annual average salaries for assistant hotel managers were approximately $30,000 in 1989; those in large hotels averaged more than $40,000 in the same year; general managers averaged $53,000. Salaries were dependent on a person's range of responsibilities, duties, experience, and size of hotel.

Professional Associations

1. The American Hotel and
   Motel Association (AH&MA)
   1201 New York Avenue, N.W.
   Washington, D.C. 20005

7. HUMAN RESOURCE MANAGERS/ TRAINING SPECIALISTS

As a more culturally diverse work force emerges with the pending entrance of more women and minority workers, and international business competition becomes more keen, human resources managers will increasingly become key corporate players. In their bidding to help companies attract and keep the best employees, these professionals will assist companies in creating environments of inclusion for all workers, and come up with innovative ways to make corporate life more attractive. Those managers who are on the cutting edge of dealing with a culturally diverse work force will find good opportunities on the human resources management team.

In much the same way, training specialists will assume a vital role in Corporate America, because there is a work force that must be motivated and trained in new technologies. These professionals must develop training materials, workshops, and courses to retain and ready the work force for stiff domestic and international competition. Their companies' survival depends upon their innovativeness. There will also be a growing business for outside corporate trainers, who will provide companies with up-to-the-minute training seminars.

Education And Training

The field of human resources, which was once called personnel, is diverse in terms of duties and responsibilities, and so are the educational requirements for entrance into it. Entry-level positions are usually filled by recent college graduates, who have majored in personnel administration, business, liberal arts, or a technical field. Colleges and universities now offer baccalaureate degree programs in personnel and labor relations, personnel administration or personnel management; some offer certificate programs in training and development. You should also take any courses that will help you develop good people management and communications skills. Teachers, social workers, counselors, and psychologists have found positions in corporate human resources or employee assistance, or career/strategic planning programs.

SALARIES

The *Occupational Outlook Handbook* reported that personnel or human resources managers had median salaries of $29,000 in 1988 with the highest earners making over $52,000 a year.

For more information contact:

1. American Society for Personnel Administration
    606 N. Washington Street
    Alexandria, Virginia 22314
2. American Society for Training and Development
    4 King Street
    Alexandria, Virginia 22313
    (703) 683-8100

8. ENGINEERS

Engineers' designs have changed the quality of our lives: we have been propelled into space; travelled safely on highways, across bridges, by planes, or rapid transit systems; communicated by telephone, radio, and television; had our lives prolonged by advanced technologies; kept warm in winter or cool in summer, because of heating and air conditioning machinery, etc. For this vital work, engineers are some of the highest paid professionals, and the engineering field offers a wide choice of challenging career opportunities.

According to the Department of Labor, Bureau of Labor Statistics, engineering is the second largest profession, and employment in the field is expected to increase faster than the average of all occupations. There are 25 major specialties in the field including agricultural; aerospace, aeronautical, and astronautical; architectural; ceramic; chemical; civil; computer; electrical; environmental health; geophysical; mechanical; metallurgical; nuclear; ocean; petroleum, etc.

Education And Training

If you want an entry-level or beginning engineering position, you must have a bachelor's degree in the field. Some science or mathematics majors are eligible for a few positions. If you attend a two- or -four year engineering technology program, you may obtain a position similar to that of the baccalaureate graduate, but employers may consider your preparation that of a technician's.

To work as an engineer, you must be licensed. Many engineers are registered and registration procedures require graduation from an accredited degree program and the passing of a state examination.

Salaries

Recent engineering graduates continue to make top starting salaries. According to *Recruiting Trends* starting salaries for June 1990 college graduates with bachelor's degrees was $33,380 for those in chemical engineering,

$32,107 for electrical engineering, $32,256 for mechanical engineering, and $27,707 for civil engineering.

For more information contact:
1. Jets-Guidance
   1420 King Street, Suite 405
   Alexandria, Virginia 22314
2. Society of Women Engineers
   345 E. 47th Street
   New York, New York 10017
3. The Accreditation Board of Engineering
      and Technology
   345 E. 47th Street
   New York, New York 10017

9. ACCOUNTANTS

Before or on April 15th, we all trudge to our accountants to get our Federal, state, and local taxes computed. It is this particular time of year when accountants receive the most public acclaim. However, they work year 'round and are the vital professionals who provide financial information to businesses and other organizations. Some are public, management, or government accountants; still others specialize in internal auditing. According to experts, international accountants will enjoy the best career opportunities in the coming years. However, the Department of Labor has reported that employment prospects for all accountants and auditors will grow faster than the average for all occupations through the year 2000.

One of the benefits of the accounting field is that accountants work in all or most industries. You can, therefore, combine two of your career loves. For example, let's say that you have majored in accounting, but also have an interest in the advertising industry. You can work as an accountant for an advertising agency.

Education And Training

If you want an entry-level accounting position in a public accounting or business company, you must have a bachelor's degree in accounting or a related field. Some companies may require a candidate to have a master's degree in accounting or a master's degree in business administration with a specialization in accounting.

If you want to become a Certified Public Accountant (CPA), you must be licensed by a state board of accountancy and also have a certificate. According to your state's educational guidelines for becoming a CPA, you may be required to have specified years of work experience, or a bachelor's or masters degree. Eight states require or will require CPA candidates to have 150 semester hours of college education or one year beyond the bachelor's degree.

For certification, you must successfully pass a four-part Uniform CPA Examination, and there are varying amounts of required public accountancy work experience according to individual state guidelines. Professional associations also have voluntary certification for its professionals including the Certified Internal Auditor (CIA), conferred by the Institute of Internal Auditors; the Certified Information Systems Auditor (CISA), conferred by the EDP Auditors Association; and the Certificate in Management Accounting (CMA), from the National Association of Accountants (NAA).

Salaries

Recruiting Trends reported that June 1990 accounting graduates with bachelor's degrees had estimated starting salaries of $27,051.

For more information contact:

1. American Institute of Certified Public Accountants

1211 Avenue of the Americas
New York, New York 10036-8775
2. National Association of Accountants
10 Paragon Drive
Montvale, New Jersey 07645
3. National Society of Public Accountants
and Accreditation
Council for Accountancy
1010 North Fairfax Street
Alexandria, Virginia 22314
4. The Institute of Internal Auditors
249 Maitland Avenue
Altamonte Springs, Florida 32701
5. The EDP Auditors Association
PO Box 88180
Carol Stream, Illinois 60188-0180

10. ENTREPRENEURS

Some experts have purported that this is the decade of
the small business owner. As more and more people tackle
the entrepreneurial trial, growth in this area is predict-
able. There are many different types of businesses to
pursue: furniture rental stores; consulting businesses;
employment agencies, nurse's registries; salad bars; art
galleries; flower shops; publishing companies; tennis and
racquetball clubs; frozen yogurt shops; secretarial services;
carpet cleaning services; t-shirt shops; flea markets; training seminars; and the list goes on. Today, if you have a good
idea, put enough energy into it, and can finance your
venture, you can join the thousands of successful owners.

Education And Training

There are no specific educational or training requirements for owning most businesses. High school drop-outs
and graduates, housewives, college students and

graduates, and those with doctorates have started successful businesses. In many cases, all you need for business ownership is a good idea and some strong management techniques. However, if you want to open a consultant business, you must have some expertise in your chosen field.

Salaries

This is a field where salaries are unlimited. You can gross from one dollar to over a million dollars a year. It depends on the strength of your business idea, how well motivated you are, and resiliency of the economy.

For more information contact:
1. Small Business Administration
   1441 L Street, N.W.
   Washington, D.C. 20416
2. American Women's Economic Development
      Corporation
   60 East 42nd Street
   New York, New York 10015

SOURCES: *The Occupational Outlook Handbook*
(Department of Labor,
Bureau of Labor Statistics).
Recruiting Trends by L. Patrick Scheetz,
Michigan State University.

9

EXPLORING COMMON JOB SEARCH TECHNIQUES

You have decided what to do, revealed your goals, uncovered your various skills, and completed your career research. It is now time to consider how to look for a job. You've worked hard in assessing your strengths and abilities and where you would like to use them. Now you must work harder in getting your perfect job. After all, finding a job is a full-time job which can take from six months to a year.

There are several ways that people look for a job: answering classified ads in the newspapers or job postings; following through on referrals by friends and/or relatives; going to a company or organization's human resources department and filling out applications; asking for placement from a private or state employment agency or executive recruitment firm. Although many people have received jobs this way, there are many pitfalls in these job seeking methods. Let's look at the problems of each one.

Classified Newspaper Ads

First, answering classified newspaper ads is a very popular way to look for a job. It is so easy to look in the newspaper, select a job, and hope for an interview. Unfortunately, if you don't have the specific qualifications for a listed job, you probably won't have much luck with getting an interview call.

Let's take this example—you may see this ad: "Firm needs 5 drafters with minimum of five years experience. Must have computer aided drafting (CAD), and architectural and mechanical drafting experience. Good salary with benefits." If you have three and a half years in the field, and only know mechanical drafting, you probably won't get called in for an interview. In today's competitive job market, you must have the specific job specifications or more to successfully use classified newspaper ads.

Because the job market is so competitive, another problem with classified ads is the number of people who respond to them. You are definitely *not* the only one who is looking at the ad. There are, possibly, hundreds of other people who qualify for a position, and have also answered the ad. Unless your qualifications are impressive, it will be undoubtedly difficult for you to get an interview. On the other hand, if your qualifications perfectly match the ad's desired ones, you have a good chance for acceptance.

Another problem with answering classified ads is that only a small percentage of jobs are advertised in newspapers. Many job openings never reach the newspaper. A job opening usually originates in the mind of the employer who must fill the slot. People in the department are next told about a job opening, and they let their interested friends know about it. If the job isn't filled by this word-of-mouth method, the employer will let the human resources department know. Human resource staffers look through their files and refer qualified candidates to the employer. If no qualified candidate is hired, the job is put in the newspaper. It is through this time consuming and tedious procedure that the bulk of classified ads land in newspapers.

A fourth reason that classified ads don't work for the majority of job seekers is there are false ads or ads placed by people who don't have immediate job openings. You might wonder why someone would do this. There are various reasons. Some employment agencies want certain employees for future job assignments, and place ads to see what type of candidates are available. Other agencies place ads to lure unsuspecting job seekers to take other positions. If you read an ad that sounds too good to be true, it probably is.

Job Postings

Because of affirmative action guidelines and union contracts, many jobs have to be posted. Sometimes this is just a procedure because a candidate has already been chosen for the job. Since, in many cases, the chosen candidate is someone who works in the department or is a friend of the employer's, job postings sometimes are just formalities.

Of course, all posted jobs have not been "filled." If you know of a legitimate posted position, apply for it. Sometimes this is an excellent way to get a job.

Referrals By Friends And Relatives

There are scores of job seekers who get jobs through friend and relative referrals. However, upon closer examination, these referrals were for entry-level positions or jobs in certain fields *i.e.,* construction, teaching, counseling. More upper echelon jobs are found through more sophisticated networking through professional networks or contacts. It is fine to get a job through a friend or relative referral, just make sure it is a job that you want and one which will use all of your skills.

Human Resources Departments

Some job seekers go to a company's human resources department, fill out an application, and are able to land jobs. If you want an entry-level position, this is a valuable way to look for a job. However, if you want a higher level position, you may be doing yourself a disservice to solely rely on this method.

Private Or State Employment Agencies

Most job seekers need assistance in their job searches and seek help from private employment agencies. Some of these agencies charge a fee for their assistance; others are paid by employers. Since these agencies must generate business from employers and their business survival depends upon employer satisfaction, they tend to be more employer than job-seeker oriented. Because their reputations depend upon it, they want to place the best candidate with an employer. This often means that many job seekers won't be successfully placed by these agencies.

If an employer hires an agency to place a candidate with ten years of secretarial experience and word processing skills, the agency will try to match that request. If you have only five years of secretarial experience with limited word processing skills, you probably won't get a chance to go on the interview.

If you want a secretarial, clerical, receptionist, bookkeeping position, you can successfully utilize private employment agencies. If you have a doctorate and are a woman, you will probably be asked to demonstrate your typing skills, and should quickly exit the office. As many television programs have shown, if you are a minority or

older person, you can face discrimination from some
agencies.

State employment agencies have helped many people
become placed in positions. However, many of them are
most helpful with placements in entry-level secretarial or
clerical, etc. They can also provide great assistance in
steering job seekers to Federal, state, and local positions.

Executive Recruitment Firms Or "Headhunters"

The average job seeker doesn't know the function of an
executive recruitment firm or "headhunter." They are
usually contracted by employers to locate certain types of
employees who are doing well in their fields, and persuade
them to switch jobs. Some agencies place unsolicited job
candidates, but this is often not their primary function. If
you have impressive credentials, you may find an executive
recruiter who is willing to place you.

10

MAPPING YOUR OWN JOB SEARCH

Taking matters into your own hands is one of the best ways to look for a job. Rather than being passive or letting someone else do the work for you, you should determine the where, what, why, who of your job campaign.

"Where"

To know the "where" of your job campaign, you should calculate where it is you want to work. Do you want to work for a small, medium, or large company? A small company may offer more ground floor opportunities for career advancement. On the other hand, a medium-sized company may offer a better salary. But a larger company may have the best training program. Only you can decide which is the best type of company for you.

The "where" can include geographic locations. Are you willing to relocate for better job opportunities? Which places would be more suitable? Do you only want to work in your city or will you commute to a neighboring town or state?

Geographic location is very important to the job seeker because it can mean career happiness. For example, you may find the perfect job which requires a two-hour commute. Are you willing to make the sacrifice? Or your perfect job may be located in a far away state. Can you relocate away from family and friends? There are people who just want to work in their neighborhoods, and would be miserable in other locales. It depends upon you and your personal preferences as to the best geographic location.

The "where" can be the industry in which you want to work. Many industries employ different types of workers within it. For example, the record industry employs secretaries, clerks, attorneys, paralegals, computer programmers, sales people, bookkeepers, human resources staffers, accountants, marketing specialists and others. So, it is very important to know the industry in which you want to work. You may find a more exciting career opportunity in one industry over another one.

Where you work can mean determining the department or agency you prefer. For example, you may want to work for ABC company as a secretary, but the public relations office is more exciting than the finance one. Or you may want to work as a clerk in the human resources department of an agency rather than in the accounting one.

"What"

What do you want to do in your new job? For example, if you want to work for a Federal, state, or local government agency, there are literally hundreds of positions that are available to people of varying educational backgrounds. Do you know what the available positions are within a company or agency for someone with your qualifications?

Do you want to work in a position which contributes directly to the profits of the company, or a support staff which will experience the first lay-off rounds during cutbacks?

It is very tragic that many job seekers settle for jobs when more suitable ones are within their grasps. It is up to to you to decide what type of job is best.

"Why"

Next, you should decide why you want to work in your future company and position. Are you generally interested in both or do you just want to take the first available opening? The stronger you feel about your future company and position, the better chance you have in getting the job.

"Who?"

Who do you want to work for? The chief executive officer, the senior vice-president, etc.? With whom will you get the best career mobility and opportunities? Most job seekers never give a thought to whom they will work, but determining this can make or break your chances for career happiness.

What personality would you like your boss to have? Fair, honest, tolerant, moody, creative, stifling? You may think that you don't have any control over who you work for, but you do. If you take your time, ask the right questions, and make solid decisions about your future, you can have control.

The "who" also has to do with who you are and what you would like out of the future. Are you a creative person? Certainly, a boring and unproductive job would make you miserable. Are you shy and retiring? A public relations position or one that requires constant public contact may not be for you. If you are free spirited, you may not be suited for a nine-to-five job or one where you are desk bound.

Mapping Your Job Search

After answering these soul-searching questions, use the information to map your own job search. First, make a list of possible companies or organizations where you would like to work. Use the information from your career research notes or continue to talk to people in the field. Look in the yellow pages for company addresses or telephone numbers, or write to your local chamber of commerce for a list of local companies.

Don't forget to ask your local librarian to help. Often, libraries have directories of certain types of organizations. For example, if you want to work for a social service organization, it is possible that your library may have a directory of these local agencies.

Have you narrowed down where you want to work, and have telephone numbers and addresses for your prospective employers? Now, let your fingers do the walking. You may be afraid to make "cold calls," but muster up the courage.

Below is a sample conversation:

You: "Hello, my name is Barbara Jones. May I speak to the person in charge of the word processing department?"

ABC Company: "Yes. That is Ms. Kuffman. I'll transfer you."

Ms. Kuffman: "Lois Kuffman."

You: "Ms. Kuffman, my name is Barbara Jones. Do you have any available job openings for word processing operators? I have five years experience in the field and know the latest word processing programs."

Ms. Kuffman: "As a matter of fact, we have two openings that will be available in a week. Send me your resume."

Believe it or not, it can be just that simple to locate a job opening. There have been job seekers who have found jobs with one telephone call. Others have gone through every name in the telephone book and located a job opening on the fortieth try.

Although it may be easy to locate jobs or positions through this innovative method, you must be able to sell yourself to get the job. You will have two opportunities to sell yourself: by presenting a good resume and cover letter and having a good interview. In *Chapters 11* through *16*, you will learn how to write a resume and cover letter that will open doors; in *Chapter 17*, you will learn how to master the interview.

11

PREPARING FOR YOUR RESUME

Unfortunately, many of you don't know how to write a good resume. It wasn't taught to you in school, and you haven't a clue as to how to develop a good one. Yet, a resume is the key marketing tool that can make your career a reality. It can also make or break your chances for getting the perfect position. So, don't get caught without a great resume.

Before you write your resume, take a few minutes to do some resume preparation and planning. Take out a piece of paper and write the following in Table 5: your present and last job titles; your job duties at each position; the work achievements for each position (refer to *Chapter* 6); volunteer work; your educational training in schools, colleges, vocational trade schools and other institutions; honors and achievements. Be sure to include when you did each of these activities. Later, you will use this information to create a good resume.

TABLE 5

My Present Position (including dates):

_____

My Present Employer:

_____

My Duties: _____

_____

_____

_____

_____

_____

_____

_____

_____

_____

My Work Achievements: _____

_____

_____

_____

_____

_____

_____

_____

My Last Position (including dates): _____

_____

My Former Employer: _____

_____

My Duties: _____

_____

_____

_____

_____

_____

_____

_____

_____

My Work Achievements: _____

_____

_____

_____

_____

_____

_____

(Note: You should write the job title, duties, and work achievements for each paid and non-paid position that you have had.)

My Educational Institutions (including dates and addresses):

Colleges (1) _____

(2) _____

(3) Major and courses that apply to your future job: _____

_____

_____

_____

_____

_____

(4) Extracurricular Activities: _____

_____

_____

_____

_____

_____

(5) Honors and Achievements: _____

_____

_____

_____

(Note: If you didn't graduate, list your courses.)

High School: _____

       (1) List courses which are applicable to your future career: _____

_____

_____

       (2) Extracurricular Activities: _____

_____

_____

       (3) Honors and Achievements: _____

_____

Vocational Schools: _____

       (1) List courses which are applicable to your future career: _____

_____

_____

       (2) Honors and Achievements: _____

_____

Special Skills: _____

_____

_____

Honors and Achievements (including dates): _____

_____

Professional Associations Or Civic Groups: _____

_____

_____

12

THE CHRONOLOGICAL RESUME

After you have completed your resume preparation exercise, you must decide which will be the best resume for you. Will you use the chronological, functional, or combination one?

In this chapter, we will look at the chronological resume which lists your work and educational experiences in reverse chronological order, or present or last job first. Although many job seekers use the chronological resume, it should be primarily used by job seekers who want the same or a similar position, or a supervisory one in their present or another field. For example, if you are a secretary who wants to move into another secretarial position, use the chronological resume. Or, if you are a secretary who wants to move into an administrative assistant's position, use the chronological one. A college student, who is a new job market entrant, should also use this format.

It is now time to write your chronological resume. First, take another look at your general, hidden, and transferable skills. Since you have some idea of the skills needed for your future career from the "Transferable Skills" exercise in *Chapter 5*, look at your entire skills list and match the skills that you have.

Review your work achievments in *Chapter 6*. Do you have any that will make a future employer take notice? Are any of your achievements directly applicable to your new career?

One key point to remember in resume writing is that a resume isn't an autobiography. It is a short synopsis of your work and educational history. Since it is for the employer, it should be written with him or her in mind. In other words, write your resume from the employer's perspective and not yours. Ask yourself, if I was an employer who wanted to hire someone for *X* position, what would I want that person to have in terms of training, work experience and/or honors and achievements.

Look at **Table 6**. First, write your name, address (including street, apartment number, city, state, and zip code) and both work and home telephone numbers, or a telephone number where you can be reached during the day. After all, an employer won't send you a telegram to ask you to come in for an interview.

Next, write your job objective, but only if you are clear about what position you want. For example, many job seekers list their job objectives as: "Want position where I can utilize my talents and skills." Doesn't everyone want to use their talents and skills in a position? Another vague job objective is: "Want position where I can benefit the company and work to my highest level of achievement." Again, doesn't everyone want to do that?

Your job objective should be specific: "Want position as management trainee for mid-size Northeastern bank" or "Want position as meeting planner for large hotel chain." Or, you should be as Janet Wilson is in the **Table 6**: "Executive Management Trainee with large California department store."

Many people ask whether to put their job or educational experiences first in the next section of their resumes. The general rule is that if you are 21 years old or older and have been in the job market, you should put your work experience first.

The exceptions would be for college students who are entering the job market, or people who work in fields where education heavily counts, or for those who want to stress an impressive educational experience. In the case of Janet, who is a graduating college student, with some impressive internship, she places this information first. Because she has such outstanding achievements in her cooperative and internship, she wants the employer to see this first.

If you are using your work experience first, you should start with your present or last employer. Generally speaking, your work dates should go on the left side of your resume, and they should be correct and complete: "September 1987-June 1989." On the right side, write your employers' names and addresses, your job titles and duties. It is not necessary to put the employer's full address, phone numbers, or the name of your supervisor. Janet puts "Lofton Department Store, Anchorage, Alaska and Tres Jolie Chic Salon, Paris, France." If your future employer wants a reference, you can give it to him or her at a later date.

In the job duties section, you should review your skills, and particularly stress those needed for your new career. Include your work achievements. For example, it is not adequate to write "was retailing intern at ABC store," but rather, "was retailing intern at ABC store. Helped increase sales 30% by assisting buyer in merchandise selection." Or, don't just write "worked as floral designer for florist," but, "worked as floral designer. Created floral designs with balloons that increased business by 50%. Received appreciation letter from owner."

Look at Janet Wilson's achievements: "Helped manage staff of 20 people; gave input to buyer which helped increase consumers' purchases by 30%."

Next, list your present or last educational institution. Be sure to include complete attendance dates at each institution's name and address, but only use the city and state in the address.

If you have taken any applicable high school or college courses, list those that are applicable to your future position. For instance, let's say your future goal is to be a word processing operator, and you have an associate's degree in the field, list your degree and courses. And include any of your extracurricular activities or academic honors.

If you have any "Special Skills" or "Honors or Achievements," or "Professional or Civic Associations," insert them. For example, if you have typing, word processing, or computer skills, put them in the "Special Skills" section. In the "Honors or Achievements" section, list any awards or accomplishments (including the dates when you received them) such as "Named 'Salesperson of the Year'." And you should list any professional groups to which you belong, such as "National Secretaries Association International."

The last section on your resume should be "References." Simply write: "Will be furnished upon request." It is not necessary to write a complete list of your references.

TABLE 6

CHRONOLOGICAL RESUME

Janet Wilson
3440 Kinecaid Drive
Los Angeles, California 98404
(212) 666-6457 (Home)

JOB OBJECTIVE: **Executive Management Trainee** with large California department store chain.

WORK EXPERIENCE:
September 1987-
June 1989

Lofton Department Store, Anchorage, Alaska.
Assistant to the Buyer
Was hired for "Top Achievers in Scholastic Retailing" Cooperative Program which is competitive and open to twenty national winners. Worked as Assistant to the Buyer in $350 million a year Misses Dress Department. Developed price structure and sales projections with Buyer's assistance.

Helped manage sales staff of 20 people. Was in charge of sales force during Buyer's and Assistant Buyer's absences.

June 1986- September 1986	**Tres Jolie Chic Salon**, Paris, France. *Assistant to the Buyer* Participated in international internship in Europe. Worked for boutique with $1.1 million yearly sales volume. Traveled with Buyer to Orient, Italy, and England to purchase clothes. Gave input to Buyer which helped increase consumers' purchases by 30%

EDUCATION:
September 1985-
Present

Institute of Fashion Design and Technology, Los Angeles, California.
Will receive Bachelor of Science degree in Retailing and Apparel Design in June 1991.

Extracurricular Activities: Corresponding Secretary for Student Government; President, National Society of Retailing majors.

SPECIAL SKILLS:

Knowledge of WordPerfect, Lotus 1-2-3.
Fluent in French and Spanish.

HONORS AND ACHIEVEMENTS:

National Dean's List (four semesters).

REFERENCES:

Will be furnished upon request.

13

THE FUNCTIONAL RESUME

If you are a career changer or someone who has been out of the job market or has an unsteady work history, you should use the functional resume which highlights the skills you have for a particular position. Because employment dates can be left out of the functional resume, you can focus on your skills, and/ or de-emphasize your unsteady work history.

If you are writing the functional resume, you must determine the skills needed for your future career, and group them into skill areas (*See Table 7*). To help you, refer to the transferable skills exercise in *Chapter 5*. Remember, this resume should be used only by career changers or people who want to highlight certain aspects of their work experience, or by those who have an unsteady work history or who have been out of the job market for some time.

Look at Mary Lynn Fineman's resume. She is a housewife who has been out of the job market for a few years, but has some impressive former work experience in hospital administration. She has grouped her work skills ino two areas: "Hospital Administration And Management" and "Health Care Program Development." In glancing at her resume, the first thing you notice is her outstanding work achievements, so she has, thus, successfully de-emphasized her years out of the job market.

If you have an unsteady work history with one or two years out of the job market, you can also successfully use the functional resume like Mary. Start by determining the skill area or areas needed for your future job.

Focus on your skills and work achievements that make you eligible for this position. For example, say you are a bookkeeper who has been out of the job market for several years, but want to highlight your bookkeeping career. The major skill area that you should highlight will be "Bookkeeping." If you have extensive "Computer Bookkeeping Skills," then this could be another major skill area. Your functional resume would be divided in half with your "Bookkeeping" skills on the firt half and your "Computer Bookkeeping Skills" on the bottom.

To write the functional resume correctly, you must ask yourself: "If I was an employer who wants to hire an X, what major skill areas would I want that person to have?" If you want a word processing position, your future employer might want you to have the following major skill areas: "Word Processing," "Administrative Assistance," and "Secretarial."

TABLE 7

FUNCTIONAL RESUME

MARY LYNN FINEMAN

34456 Tenth Avenue
Kansas City, Missouri 60708-9878
(607) 555-5512—Residence

MAJOR SKILL AREAS:

HOSPITAL ADMINISTRATION AND MANAGEMENT

Was Assistant Hospital Administrator for Providence Hospital (a 300-bed facility) in Kansas City. Helped oversee budget of $240 million. Coordinated daily operations and managed 300 staff members. Supervised twenty-five department heads and workers in Obstetrics-Gynecology, Nursing, Respiratory Therapy, Medical Records, Neurology, Dermatology, Human Resources, Buildings and Grounds, etc. Planned and conducted orientation program for senior level management staff, and wrote training materials.

HEALTH CARE PROGRAM DEVELOPMENT

Coordinated Volunteer Program activities for Edward E. Bates Hospital, a 400-bed facility in Kansas City. Supervised 300 volunteers. Developed program in its initial stages and selected four full-time staff members. Designed promotional materials to recruit volunteers and received largest response in hospital's history. Created data base management system of volunteers.

EDUCATION:

September 1985-
June 1988

Tarnac College, Kansas City, Missouri. Received Master's in Health Administration.

September 1974-
June 1978

University of Missouri at Kansas City, Kansas City, Missouri. Awarded Bachelor of Science degree in Biology.

OTHER TRAINING:

1988-1989

Cumberland College, Kansas City, Missouri.
Received certificate in "Organizational Development and Management."

HONORS AND ACHIEVEMENTS:

1983

Awarded "Employee of the Year" at Edward E. Bates Hospital for outstanding contribution to the Volunteers' Program.

SPECIAL SKILLS:

Knowledge of computers and data based management programs.

REFERENCES:

Will be furnished upon request.

14

THE COMBINATION RESUME

The combination resume is a combination of the chronological and functional resume, and should be used by career changers who want to highlight their skills for a new position as well as chronological work experience. However, the combination resume should only be used by people who have steady work experience in a particular field or if their chronological work history complements the skill areas that they have highlighted.

Since this resume is a combination of the chronological and functional resumes, the first section should highlight the skills needed or the ones that you want to highlight for your new position. The second section should give your chronological work and educational history.

Look at Robert Dells' resume in *Table 8*. He is a Human Resources Technician, but his title is misleading. He is actually involved with a great deal of administration and management, but his title makes him seem like a paraprofessional. To overcome this, he uses the combination resume to highlight his skills and work achievements, and de-emphasize his job title.

A career changer may also want to use the combination resume to highlight certain skills and not stress his or her chronological work experience. Or a person who wants to move up to a higher level position may use the combination resume to highlight skills not reflected in his or her job description or title.

Now, start writing your resume. For more information on resume writing, read *How to Write A Resume* by Elza Dinwiddie Boyd.

TABLE 8

COMBINATION RESUME

ROBERT DELLS
30 West Temple Drive
Phoenix, Arizona 23456
(303) 658-9899 — Business
(303) 876-5544 — Residence

MAJOR SKILL AREAS:

HUMAN RESOURCES/PERSONNEL

Was Human Resources Technician for large, 10,000 employee A.G. Riff Company in Phoenix. Recruited, interviewed, administered clerical testing, prepared job descriptions, and surveyed salaries. Designed and implemented departmental "Quiet Hours" to allow staff to do one hour of uninterrupted paper-work which resulted in 30% more efficiency. Formalized special internal hiring procedures for job applicants which made for better employer/employee matches, and received outstanding bonus, and "Letter of Merit" from C.E.O.

Instituted Employee Assistance program for employees with drug, alcohol, and personal problems which has helped reduce absenteeism by 50%. Implemented the establishment of company on-site gym for employees with work-related stress problems.

**MAJOR WORK
HISTORY:**

September 1989-
Present

A.G. Riff Company, Phoenix, Arizona
Human Resources Technician

August 1987-
September 1989

Lincoln Plastics Company, Phoenix, Arizona
Personnel Assistant

EDUCATION:
1983-1989

University of Arizona, Phoenix, Arizona.
Awarded Bachelor of Science degree in Personnel Management.

**PROFESSIONAL
ASSOCIATIONS:**

Member of the American Society for Personnel Administration.

REFERENCES:

Will be furnished upon request.

15

RESUME PROBLEM AREAS

Since you have been given the tools, you should be able to write a good resume. However, there are several problem areas that many job seekers overlook when in writing their resumes. Most of these problems are usually in three areas: resume appearance, work history, and educational experiences.

Many people think of resume writing as drudgery, to get over with as quickly as possible. By doing so, they fail to edit, revise, or put in key selling points. To help you present the best possible resume, look below, and check your resume for these problem areas:

RESUME PROBLEM AREAS

Appearance

1. If you want a $20,000, $50,000, or $100,000 job, you should have a $20,000, $50,000, or $100,000 resume. In other words, make sure your resume looks professional and neat. This means that there should be no grammatical or spelling errors, erasures or white-outs, etc.

2. Your resume should say you are a professional who cares about every document that goes out under your name. Therefore, it should be professionally typed or done on a word processing computer, and copied onto good stationery. Use different typefaces, to create an interesting format. And make sure the information on your resume isn't cluttered.

3. Unless you are a college professor or other type of professional where employers prefer lengthy resumes, write a one or two page resume. However, the length of your resume can depend upon industry preferences. For example, personnel people prefer or require the one page format. In other industries, the one or two page resume is appropriate. Do some research and find out the preferred resume length for your future industry.

   When you use the one page resume, remember to include all relevant information. Some job seekers, for instance, are so eager to fit their resume into the one page format that they leave out many of their job duties and achievements. If it takes two pages to adequately explain your work and educational history, use the extra page.

Work And Educational Experiences

1. Since your resume isn't an autobiography, use only relevant work experiences, skills, and training that apply to your future job. For example, it is not necessary to cite all of your summer high school jobs. Include only relevant work history.

2. Be truthful on your resume. Many employers do employee traces to see whether a person has made truthful statements on his or her resume. So, make sure your employment dates, employers, and skills are correct. In the area of educational institutions, make sure you don't lie about having a degree or

credential, or attending a certain school.

3. There are many things that shouldn't be included on your resume: health status, weight, marital status, number of children, age, supervisor's names, hobbies, etc. When put on a resume, many of these things can open up illegal questions during the interview.

  For example, let's say that you are a woman and have listed your marital status as single with two children. In an interview, an employer could say: "I see that you have two small children. You know that young children are always getting sick or can't get ready in the mornings. Will this affect your coming to or being late for work?" If this woman had excluded this information from her resume, the interviewer's questioning might have been different.

4. Regardless of what the want ad says, leave out your salary. In most cases, prematurely disclosing salary information generally hurts the applicant in future salary negotiations.

16

WRITING THE "EMPLOYER PERFECT" COVER LETTER

Now, it's time to write your cover letter. Since it's usually the first item that an employer sees, make sure it properly sells you. To successfully write a cover letter, you must take three things into consideration: 1. the position you want; 2. the person to whom you are addressing the letter; 3. what you want to highlight in it.

First, let the employer know the position that you want and how you found out about it i.e want ads, referrral, etc. Then in synopsis form, highlight your applicable work experience, skills and training. Finally, tell the person how to reach you and whether you will call in a week or few days to learn about his or her disposition on the matter. Be sure to type your cover letter on your best stationery, and never handwrite a cover letter or resume or both may end up in the trash basket. For an example of a cover letter, see **Table 9.**

TABLE 9

COVER LETTER

Mrs. Carlton Reese,
Supervisor
Child Welfare Bureau
6743 West Long Street
Chicago, Illinois 30211-9876

Dear Mrs. Reese:

I read your classified ad for a Social Worker in Sunday's newspaper. In the belief that the Child Welfare Bureau is always looking for a Social Worker with a record of strong accomplishments, you may be interested in my background:

- I have worked as a Social Worker in various capacities with the Illinois Human Resources Administration. Last year, I was promoted to Senior Social Worker based on my performance of placing abandoned and foster children;
- The *Chicago Sun Times* recently cited me for outstanding work in foster care;
- Of special interest, I began my career as a Case Investigator for H.R.A. and positively concluded 90% of my cases.

In performing my work, I have incorporated many of the social work skills from my graduate work at Loyola University. Because Social Work is an expanding and dynamic field, I am pursuing a doctorate in the field at the University of Chicago.

I am currently looking for a challenging work situation, and feel your position sounds stimulating. My telephone number and address are included in the enclosed resume. I will contact you in a week to arrange an appointment.

Sincerely,

Doris Walker

17

SELLING YOURSELF IN THE INTERVIEW

As with a resume, you must prepare for an interview. To adequately sell yourself in the interview, you must know several things: 1. to whom are you selling yourself; 2. what you want to accomplish; 3. what makes you marketable.

To determine whom you are selling yourself to, you should know something about your future company. Go back and review your company and industry notes. What type of company is it? In what industry is it? How does the company rank in terms of other companies in the industry? What is its mission? What are the company's profits and losses? What are its future trends or product developments? Is the company small, medium, or large?

The desired result of your interview is to get the position. What is your targeted position? What skills, training, or experience do you need for the position? What are the job's future career and mobility opportunities? How does it rank in the corporate or organizational hierarchy—senior management, management, supervisory, or worker status? How much does the position pay? What is the maximum salary paid for the position?

What do you have to offer the company? What are your skills, work achievements, training, and work experiences which qualify you for the position? What type of worker are you? What are your strengths and weaknesses?

If you can answer these questions, you have conquered half the battle of interview success. But you may want to explore different ways to handle interview situations:

1. When they ask about your knowledge of the company?

Here is your opportunity to let the interviewer know that your career research is thorough. If you have done your research, you can converse with the interviewer very intelligently. If he or she asks what you know about the company, describe the company in terms of its industry rank, type of business or service, type of products, last year's profits and losses, future products or trends, size, international developments.

2. When they ask you about the position?

Look at your research notes. What is the specific job that you want? Because many job applicants don't know what position they want, employers will be delighted to know you do.

What has attracted you to this position? Was it your educational or work history, or a long-desired career goal? What do people do in your position? You can ask how this particular position in this company compares to similar positions in the industry. You can also ask what the job duties and company goals are for the position.

3. When they ask you about yourself?

Focus on your skills that can be transferred to the desired position. Talk about your strengths as a worker—highly motivated, hardworking, disciplined, etc. If asked about yourself, talk about your training and educational experiences that have prepared you for the job. For instance, if you want a convention planning position that requires you to have word processing/computer skills, mention your course in word processing. Or if you are a college student who wants to enter a bank management training program, share the scope of your business courses with the interviewer.

Stress your work achievements. Show how there was a problem area at your present or former job, and how you solved it. Tell why you were prompted to do so, and what the results were. Try to paint a picture of yourself as a good, hard-working employee.

When an interviewer asks you to describe three or four things that will make her hire you, tell her about your qualities as a worker. When she asks about your weaknesses, make them sound like strengths. You could say, for example "many people say that I'm a workaholic. I usually stay late at the office and take work home. I know that people say 'all work and no play' isn't good, but I'm just dedicated."

When the interviewer asks about your past, never volunteer any negative information about yourself or former bosses or companies. Many interviewers persuade candidates to drop their guards, and as a result the applicant starts talking too much. Rather than give too much or negative information, watch your words.

4. When they talk money.

Don't bring up salaries or benefits until asked. However, if the interviewer never brings it up, you should ask about financial compensation.

Every job or position has a salary range, and you should know the one for your targeted position. Remember the interviewer wants to get you for the least amount. If the salary range for your position is from $19,000-$25,000, the interviewer will get points from management for hiring you at the lowest rate. So it's up to you to know the prevalent salaries in your future field. You must also analyze your skills, training, and work experience to determine what salary you merit.

For more information on interviewing, read *The No Nonsense Interview.*

APPENDIX A

READING BOOK LIST

1. Bolles, Richard N.: *The Three Boxes of Life: And How to Get Out of Them.* Ten Speed Press.

2. _____: *What Color Is Your Parachute?* Ten Speed Press.

3. Harragan, Betty Lehan: *Games Mother Never Taught You: Corporate Gamesmanship for Women.* Warner Books

4. Hill Napoleon: *Think and Grow Rich.* Fawcett.

5. Kennedy, Joyce Lain and Darryl Laramore: *Joyce Lain Kennedy's Career Book.* VGM Career Horizons.

6. Lathrop, Richard: *Who's Hiring Who.* Ten Speed Press.

7. Mandino, Og: *The Gratest Miracle in the World.* Bantam.

8. Nivens, Beatryce: *The Black Woman's Career Guide.* Anchor Press/Doubleday.

9. _____: *How To Change Careers Without Going Back to School.* Perigee Books.

10. Peale, Norman Vincent, *The Power of Positive Thinking.* Fawcett.

11. US Department of Labor, Bureau of Labor Statistics: *Dictionary of Occupational Titles*. US Government Printing Office.

12. _____: *Occupational Outlook Handbook*. US Government Printing Office.

INDEX

BEATRYCE NIVENS is an internationally known career expert. Her books include *How to Change Careers, Careers for Women Without College Degrees*, and *The Black Woman's Career Guide*. As a contributing editor for *Essence Magazine*, she wrote over 80 articles on careers. Her articles have also appeared in *Family Circle, New Woman, Black Enterprise, Black Collegian, Mademoiselle* and *Glamour*.